The Howls of Wind

A Poetry Collection by

Dedication

My first dedication is for J.S.

The one who guarded my dreams when they were fragile,who guided me toward a world of endless possibilities,
who fills my heart with gratitude and love.

With heartfelt thanks to my supportive parents, dear friends,the teachers who helped me grow,and my cherished companions:

Senna and Vicky, my golden retrievers,and Sylvia, my loyal border collie.

About Author

Windy Situ is a passionate poet and writer. She has maintained a daily writing habit for a year and a half without missing a single day, a dedication that has driven her to explore new creative horizons. Although she is currently working on six different projects, The Howls of Wind is her first published work.

Born in China, Windy moved to the United States at a young age, where she completed middle and high school in Minnesota and Kansas before graduating from the University of California, Davis. Initially, she followed her parents' advice to pursue a different field of study, but she rediscovered her love for writing in her junior year and decided to focus on English and creative writing for her graduate studies.

Her inspiration comes from a childhood friend who greatly influenced her. He once shared his dream of becoming a writer and told her, "Reading and writing spark our imagination and make us more creative." These words left a lasting impact on Windy, guiding her throughout her writing journey. Her work spans various genres, including poetry, fantasy, and a deeply personal memoir. For Windy, writing is an endless journey of self-discovery, a way to relive life's most brilliant moments and find solace in the worlds she creates.

Windy believes that true romance is "writing the poems you have yet to finish and fulfilling the dreams you have yet to achieve." She hopes that if she ever reunites with this friend, he will know that she has fulfilled his childhood dream, which has now become her own. She firmly believes that one's name and honor are earned through one's own efforts.

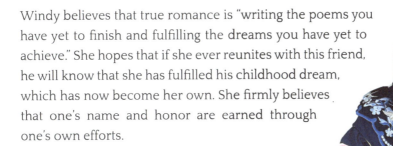

Table of Contents

01. Faith ---------- 6

02. Promising ---------- 7

03. She ---------- 8

04. Starlight ---------- 9

05. In-finite ---------- 10

06. Raven ---------- 11

07. Dawn ---------- 12

08. Turns ---------- 13

09. Hades ---------- 14

10. Heageon ---------- 15

11. Sea ---------- 17

12. Cocoon ---------- 18

13. Cross ---------- 19

14. Roof ---------- 20

15. Desert ---------- 21

16. Harbor ---------- 22

17. Hoodie ---------- 23

18. Zephyr ---------- 24

19. Once More ---------- 25

01. Reverse Scale ---------- 26

02. Tide ---------- 27

03. Beggar ---------- 28

04. Farewell ---------- 31

05. Alive ---------- 32

06. Ghost ---------- 33

07. Apple Flower ---------- 35

08. Fortnight ---------- 36

09. Shadow ---------- 37

10. Dune ---------- 39

11. Oath ---------- 40

12. Orchard ---------- 41

13. Youth ---------- 42

14. First Love ---------- 43

15. Guardian ---------- 44

16. Awaken ---------- 45

Faith

They say the moon is a perfect circle,
too slippery to hang their wishes on,
so they sleep, lifting their heads
sparing a day, then another.

They claim the sun is out of reach,
so they shun its light, lounging instead
beneath the oak's cooling shade,
where daydreams come easily,
one after another.

They argue that poetry is too arduous to craft,
a word here, a word there,
barely enough to fill a page.
Thus, they seek fleeting joys
sparing their minds from deeper ploys.

Yet, the moon builds a crescent.
Those who dare
hang their wishes on it gracefully.
The moon gently rocks the sleeping wishes—
cradles them like a baby.
The wishes gather
as the moon glows brighter,
winking with a faithful glow.

And the sun, when it reaches noon,
softly calms the sea—
its radiant, gentle touch
enfolds those who worship its warmth,
shielding the hymns of their praise.

where poetry endures through the ages,
reaching the minds of educated sages,
traveling from the Silk Road to the great Pyramids,
knotted with the veins,
of contemporary saints.

Promising

What is love?
the little girl asked.
The prince slashed all the lusting souls
that once wanted to suck her spirit out.
She sent herself to the barren desert,
and after she's strong enough,
the prince won't bear those anguishes for her anymore.
Even the greenest plant cannot survive in the Sahara.

What is love?
the little girl mused.
She holds an empty bowl
with only a few pieces of bread left in it.
She gave it to the boy,
and suddenly, a black pigeon snatched it away.
The boy, adorned in armor,
had sorrow in his eyes when he noticed the bread was gone.
The glowing weapon won't shine on peaceful land.

What is love?
the little girl blinked.
She couldn't remember if she got a Christmas tree last December,
or if any gifts were hanging on the tree,
but she cherished the note he once gave her.
It read,
"Merry Christmas, little one."
The purest snow won't fall in winter.

What is love?
the lady nodded,
with pages crafted in hand,
heavy as the prince's once armored belt.
2000 miles
and the lady smiles,
"Happy Birthday."
The precious cherry blossoms won't blossom in spring.

She

My pen's tip carries dust from Mesopotamia;
each speck tells the tale of a fallen realm.
My papers have wrinkled through ages more ancient than Zeus—
each crease like a lightning bolt on the page.

My wand stood on the ground,
Spells long awaited, with thousands around.
Yet under its weight, no magic was cast,
Only an ant, wounded and surpassed.

I've never wanted to stand atop the pyramid,
looking into a so-called clear atmosphere.
When you place your hand upon my pages,
your eyes trace each line with silent thought,
but you'll never see the faint graphite dust
on your little finger—
a precious trace of words left behind.

Go ahead and dream of Artemis playing a beautiful tune,
trapping you in the cave of great Titans.
I'm laying cozy in Elysium, drinking alone.

Starlight

Starlight, you cast—
crafted from your celestial light,
yet upon the ground,
shadows are what people see.

Rainbows, you paint across the sky—
yet on the soil beneath,
some claim they're but mere illusions,
leading nowhere, touching no heart.

Snowflakes, you bestow—
yet upon the earth,
complaints arise of the chill,
the cold seeping into bones sparks shivers.

Winds, you send—
yet at ground level,
voices murmur of obscured sight,
blurring visions and dreams alike.

Sands, you sculpt—
yet on the surface,
skeptics whisper of ancient tales,
dismissing the stories buried deep.

But for the visionaries, starlight is cast—
a bright beacon for those chasing veritas.
But for the lost-soul poets, rainbows fall—
foretelling each fortune's lore.

Snowflakes fall heavily,
shielding the realms of polar bears
and preserving life in frozen silence.
Winds, carrying whispered thoughts,
bind distant hearts with invisible threads.
Sands that spread, harbor histories,
cradling dormant memories.

In-finite

infinite snows blanket finite lands
infinite rains drench finite crops
infinite tongues shaped by finite words

thus, the land dons a pristine white cloak

thus, the crops burgeon into bloom
thus, language weaves its fantasies
escorting breaths away from fear

Raven

A raven circles, singing a witch's chant,
its eerie tones echo off the ceiling.
The priest, mid-sermon, feels the piercing rant—
disturbance veiling sacred plans.

The faithful sit stiff and still and
murmur over the disruptive shrill.
With Bibles raised as shields, their voices fill
the air to drown the sounds they wish to kill.

Yet still the raven sings its spell,
As the congregants' volume swell.
In awkward harmony, echoes dwell—
a dome of discord where they quell.

The priest shuts his tome with a roar:
"Depart, vile bird of myth and lore!"
Yet on it sings, as before,
ignoring threats of a holy war.

He wields a wand, aims with intent;
the raven twirls, the curse unbent.
Till, from the crowd, missives are sent—
a volley that the silence rent.

It flees at last to corners dim,
And peace descends on a whim.
The chamber rests, its light not grim,
a quiet veil, at hymn's end, prim.

Dawn

Hue shines dimly in their eyes.
"Rhea," they say to the sky.
The land embraces their claws,
the dirt sticks to their nails.
Their noses are wet,
and baring their death,
they snarl.

Twilight kisses the peak's edge,
but the beast's stare wanders off the peak.
Hundreds of weeks, dawn has set and faded,
Yet the hue of their eyes remains.
Through thousands of days of flow, they endure,
the hue of their eyes remains.

But the gentle touch of warmth
makes their noses wet,
cleans their claws,
relaxes their muscles,
quickens their heartbeats.
The hue of their eyes glow lilac,
as dawn comes and reflects in their eyes.
Night is their gown,
Dawn is their crown.

Turns

It's a sword, diamond-decorated,
hanging high on the honoring throne.
Not even holy kings receive the honor of wielding it,
They only worship it—days spent with priests
singing holy songs of praise at night.
It never tires of slaying flesh,
yet still will garner honored lines for centuries.

It's a worthy pen,
its cap intricately decorated with an old totem,
tipped with a statue, ancient,
a reflection of the glory of knights
who danced in the fountain's midst, blades downturned.
This pen scripts poems that gods from above pass to their offspring.

It's a rainbow-kissed plant,
bearing only two leaves,
one on the left, another on the right.
It never feels the rain's kiss,
nor experiences the storm's change,
embraced by the rainbow from the moment it was born.

And now,
the sword is wielded not in glory but in battle,
shattering the chamber walls as invaders fall.
The pen scripts not for gods but for the weary;
its words turn fallen angels away from their descent.

It is time—
to stand tall against the storm,
to face the howls of wind.

Hades

I revel in blossoms not bound to the earth,
not in the damp soil or the shadowed road's berth,
but in the ascent above, where glow unfurls
night's fleeting pearls.

Their genesis lies deep, where the concealed paths wind,
from the nadir, they climb, a spectacle to find.
Ignited in autumn's fall, to the heavens they aim,
catching late maple's glare through winter's tears, they claim.

Yes, they grow, not as flora seeking the sun's embrace,
but as embers aspiring to burst, to transcend their base.
Transforming, they seek not flora's full attire
but to dazzle briefly in a pyrotechnic choir.

Seeds remain, but seeds, in their essence true,
should you seek their legacy, let the forest guide you through.
There, amidst the emerald, find your solace or your dread—
alive with the fire's luster or in Hades' cold bed,
where all is enfolded, in silence, deeply wed.

Heageon

The medal hangs from the ceiling,
the rope brushing my very hair.
The bronze shines so brightly
its luminosity overcomes the shadow of the dungeon's wall.
Its glory pulls down the pure white hem of the lord of Heaven's dress.
The air of encouragement is so dense
it stops me from breathing.
The tension of expectation is so intense,
it seizes the nerves of every cell.
Triumph extends beyond,
lying in the depths of my reverie,
yet,
the same medal that weighs me down,
so heavy my muscles twist.

The same bronze, shining over the wall,
blinds my directional sight,
blurs every path,
darkens every garden corner,
stings the wings of bees in the yard.

The encouragement is so loud
my ears go deaf, and I hear only 'help, help.'
Expectations soared into the sky by the mighty emerald dragon,
loosen in its claw,
smashing into the dungeon,
freeing all the lusting souls once crying for freedom.

Every cell of mine begins to cry out loud—
life is what you need.

Dungeons and burdens no longer bind,
and the Goddess with a half-covered face approaches me.
Her masks are love, kindness, and destiny.
Suddenly, she speaks—
Her words: 'path,' 'trust,' 'peace,' 'calm,' 'freedom.'

She kneels next to me,
gentle as a kiss.
She murmurs, takes off her mask—
now I see her face,
She's Elpis, released from Pandora's box.
Now she whispers by my ear:

"The dungeon will hint at heaven,
and you will always have your free will.
When you think your time has come,
come to me,
release all burdens suddenly,
shed the armored coat with honors embroidered on it,
tear off your mask, like I did,
raise your scorching blade to fight,
or lay it down for a new life.
But whatever you choose,
I will be here—
in life or death,
dungeon or heaven,
you'll have a place.
It's time to see the real medals,

to see if they're worth the applause
or not worth any at all."

The heaven shall bloom,
the dungeon shall sink,
the heaven shall kill,
the dungeon shall heal.

Sea

I once said the sea was pale blue silk.
As it unfolds
the dreary place
seems a little less so
if only briefly.

Like fireworks, their smoky trails are soon forgotten
yet, in our lives, that light is transient.

I found a stillness as I watched the flickering light
that defied time. No longer
did I fear its flame would burn my fingers.

The smoke forms a dragon before it fades away.
a yard adorned with wooden chairs is
frozen in time, their secrets etched
deep in my memory, slipping from my grasp.

Now, the sea is more than just pale silk—
It's a gateway to radiant heights,
an unforgettable moment
an instant of peace beneath shadows' reign.

A joy that dispels the creeping shadows,
with a holy angel's halo bright,
guarding the beast within the night.

Since then, I've admired the sea,
for in its expanse, peace resides within me,
enduring as long as I breathe.

Cocoon

leaves sing their harmony as
morning bugs greet
the bees, who
driven by nectar's call,
pause, captivated by
my beauty

my charm lies in the rings on my wings,
in the specks that grace my
tails in the breeze stirred by my
flutter in the grandeur of
these wings, ornate and vast that
lift me to see vistas that remain
unseen by them

I soar high in the sky, gazing
at my wings in wonder, contemplating
their artistry

a gentle breeze shifts my course as I
behold the world they speak of—
below, ants march and
sprouts break through the soil, eager to explore
yet my true joy lies in my cocoon where
there is no judgment,
there is no shame.

I view the world uniquely
its blank walls hold infinite potential, a
canvas for my vibrant imagination
flourishing, rich, and peaceful

here in my cocoon,
illusion and reality converge
here, I find my peace
my own world.

a butterfly living in a cocoon,
joyful and free.

Cross

Dripping sounds resonate—
it's the pigeon's blood.
High-pitched cries pierce the air—
it's the eagle's voice.
Acid rain falls from above—
dying poppies grow scarlet stems.
Blooming roses wither—
from an out-of-season frost.
The campfire burns with a greenish glow—

The Dead Sea swallows its travelers—
but he refuses to surrender.
Buddha, with one eye open wide—
a cross, half buried in soil, half touched by the sun.
Yet—
she whispers in the barren land
with a voice only she can hear.

Roof

A roof, a ceiling, a floor,
unshaken by the wind's roar,
untouched by the pouring rain,
unfelled by thunder's refrain.
More than just a shelter,
a place where insights come from elders.

Here, lies unravel to reveal
harsh truths soften and begin to heal.
Hearts open wide, unburdened and at peace;
laughter echoes, full of glee.
The feeling, known before the door swings,
where the steadfast beacon clings.

Under this roof, shadows flee and
spiderwebs vanish, unseen by wit.
Dust settles, leaving the air clear;
a sanctuary where peace draws near.

No armored hero, nor glamorous queen,
just a human soul, tender and keen,
vulnerable with space to mend,
a quiet place where wounds can end.

A space where I can show my core,
revealing depths and even more.
Here, in this home, my heart finds rest,
embracing my humanity, unpressed.

Desert

With ears covered, she embraced the golden dunes before her,
with a heart half-pounding, she questioned reality.
With eyes blind, she lost her way on the solid path,
with layers draped, her body ceased to feel the ember.
With hair long to her waist, she numbly combed,
and as her pulse stopped longing for life, she despaired.

Deep within her, his presence stirred,
whispering softly, he said:
I'm with you, I've never left.

Her ears, once muffled, now keen and aware,
attuned to the melodies of a babbling brook,
as if she had always borne the ears of an elf,
only now ready to hear what had long been hidden.

His aura gently wielded power,
breathing life into her faltering pulse—
now, it beats with renewed strength.

As his fingers carefully lifted the crown,
he placed it with care upon her head.
Her hair, already pure as silk,
cascaded effortlessly through his fingers.

His smile healed her tear-filled eyes,
and now they reflected a sky full of shooting stars.
With tender care, he cradled her long-lost soul
until her spirit gleamed as bright as Apollo's dawn.

He reshaped hard truths into fairytales,
and now she stands having long entrusted her heart,
brimming with strength and determination.

Harbor

People once passed by with disdainful glances,
Yet the same crowd now offers praise,
endless in their blessings.

And you, unchanged,
with the same spirit,
the same fervor in your heart,
the same hands that grasp.

I chose a day to leave the restless world,
seeking solace where waters rest,
where a harbor waits with open arms,
and gentle tides hush the chaos.

There, I surrendered everything:
The fears that once anchored me,
dreams towering above the skyline,
so lofty they swayed with the sea breeze,
soaring so high they whispered to the sky.

I released the burdens that once drowned me,
the laughter that drifted like echoes,
and the ties that tethered me down.
I turned my gaze from turbulent shores,
from restless waves crashing relentlessly.

The harbor cradled me—
a sanctuary for the weary soul,
where ripples soothe with lullabies,
and waters mend with their soft embrace.
Each moment sewn with peace,
each wave a gentle stitch,
binding me to a fleeting calm.

Hoodie

"Can't see through the dark, and that's all I want,"
the boy murmurs beneath his oversized hoodie.
A woman drags his hood down—
suddenly, the eyes of the boy are uncovered.
"Look at the world!" she yells,
but the boy pulls his hoodie up again.

"Can't see through the dark, that's what I want,"
the boy murmurs beneath his big hoodie.

Ice cream drips onto his sleeve,
melted slowly by the warm wind's blow.
A gust of wind flips back his hood—
the boy's eyes open slightly.
He looks up just as a cloud shadows the sun.

"Can't see through the dark, I just want a little more time,"
the boy murmurs, hood drawn close.
The boat he was on swiftly flows,
bamboo leaves sharp as blades rustle around him;
mountains link like a canopy overhead;
he adjusts the hood just enough to see clearly.
"Wow," he exclaims, taken in by the sight.

"Can't see through the dark, that's not what I want,"
the boy finally says.
Crimson bricks gleam like mirrors;
he sits in the center of the church square.
Releasing a white pigeon from his hands,
he unties the red rope from its legs as it soars.

Smiling, he watches it disappear into the sky.

Zephyr

She breathes the air, desperate,
inhales every atom of the breeze.
Eyes closed, she tilts her head,
feeling, feeling, feeling—
it's all she desires.

The cool kiss of a spring zephyr
brushes her cheek from right to left.
The same breeze

carried her across the sea
lifted her over peaks
watched her deliver the music box
witnessed their final embrace
then parted, each on separate paths.

Now, the zephyr wraps her gently.
Her hand trembles as she writes.

People pass, denying, accepting—
Gentle, harsh—
Giving, then taking away.

A voice breaks through,
"Clean the deck and chair before you sit."
She smiles, replying,
"This is the nature I feel, where I dwell."

Once More

The novel's dedication page lies bare,
leaving blank until the final words were penned,
until the story reached its end,
until the ship of Theseus bore witness to our tale.
Only then was the dedication page truly written.

The old oath we swore,
The old wounds we bore,
memories that sank with the Titanic,
hands that never clasped.
Morpheus's prophecy we tirelessly chased,
tasks we completed with a silent grace;
they are now longing for a reunion,
an illusion as old as our journey.

The final ship sails towards the distant horizon,
carrying pieces once whole, now renewed,
narrating anew,
as daylight breaks,
I advocate the end of this illusion,
To love once more, to hold on to the world's entirety,
once more.

Reverse Scale

In dreams submerged, the dragon lay in deep repose,
with scales like armor, bathed in the ocean's deep embrace.
Around him, pearls half-buried, soft seabed's gentle close,
yet in this underwater realm, his glow does space displace.
Not by pearls' light but by his scales' ethereal grace,
dry upon the surface, yet within, a luminous race.

Scattered scales around him lie a spectacle to behold.
Fish, in awe, draw near, their curiosity quite bold.
Together, they conspire, one scale to uplift,
imagining their home adorned with this celestial gift.
Yet, the dragon's reverse scale remains elusive, adrift,
molded into his dreams, where realms and myths shift.

There, a phoenix begins to coalesce and shape,
with a subtle tilt of head and eyes in a gentle drape.
Wings unfold, encased in iron's grip, a fateful cape,
claws not sharp but soft as feathers, an escape.
Wet feathers cling to form, a transformation to anticipate,
surrounded by flames that torment her fate.

The dragon's scale, to her body, finds its way,
igniting her gaze with an eternal, bright display.
The fire becomes her ally, at her command to sway
her wings, now ablaze with orange flames, the chains fall away.
Given the dragon's reverse scale, a gift of might,
he slumbers deeply, dreaming of the phoenix's flight.

The pearls that were once surrounded by the earth are claimed,
yet, from the slumber of the dragon, a phoenix is named.
A tale of rebirth and fire from depths untamed,
where the dragon sleeps, the phoenix's glory is famed.

Tide

The boat drifted in peaceful stillness on the river,
a lotus pod settled at its bow,
touched by mud and water droplets, fresh and inviting.
A paddle plunged, stirring the boat northward,
as gentle swirls rippled out, rocking its course.
The lotus pod rolled, then fell back into the river,
where blooms seemed to welcome it, joining in their silent dance.

Now, the boat faced south, smoke rising softly in the air,
merging with the sky like a watercolor painting.
A boy's breath sent a sudden gust,
scattering the smoke's form to fading whispers,
until only a lingering scent remained,
the smoke's picture erased completely.

In a book of art, lines of poetry bloomed,
depicting lotus flowers in a radiant spread.
A flaming bird dipped low, blessing the forest below.
A firm press of graphite halted the verse,
the pencil's stub cutting the flow mid-thought,
leaving the poem unfinished,
its final lines trailing into imagination.

Beggar

I was born in a black-and-white jail,
But I heard the keepers tell stories of colors.
I wonder what color looks like—
Would it darken my black,
or purify my white?
I was set free on the Queen's birthday,
she let all the prisoners go.
I met a dinosaur,
Black in my eyes.
He promised to make me his color
if I hunted him a kangaroo.
I did, and indeed, I turned green—
The first color I had ever seen.
But I grew a tail, much like his,
dragging behind me as I walked.
Still, I spotted another color.
I wandered into a rice field,
the color of white.
I stole some corn and met a golden snub-nosed monkey,
meticulous, with empty hands.
But my green tail slowed me down—
The golden snub-nosed monkey landlord saw me.

Still, the corn was sweet,
its juice bursting on my tongue.
He wanted the corn in my hand
and promised I'd see yellow in return.
I traded the corn and witnessed yellow,
but my arms grew longer with the color,
too long to hold another ear.
I crawled awkwardly from the field
into an open land,
Where I let my body rest,
relaxing my tail and aching arms.
Facing the earth,
the smell of wet soil called me to drink.
I crawled to a dark river
and drank from its depths.
The water tasted pure,
and a swan approached.
Her white was whiter
than any field I had seen.
She drove me away from her moonlit bath
but promised me orange, like her beak,
if I brought her a fish.
I did, and she gave me orange—
but my mouth grew long,
turning into a beak like hers.

I could no longer speak my human tongue,
nor understand the language of swans.
I closed my eyes and drifted down the river
until I could see again.
There was a beggar
offering me his only bread.
I noticed his hair, black,
And his eyes, brown as walnut wood.
His smile was kind,
and he poured water into my mouth.
As I looked into his eyes,
I saw more than just color—
I saw myself.
My heart pounded,
and the colors transformed within me.
My tail dissolved,
my arms shrank,
and my mouth spoke again—
for love.

Farewell

He was a horse once, wandering the Taklimakan in desperation
Unsuited to such a barren land,
days and weeks took their toll.
His frame dwindled to mere bones,
yet those bones accumulated,
forming a mound.
Sublimely, this mound began to retain water, offering him sustenance.
From that moment forward,
he adopted the name camel,
the original name he bore as a horse
fading into oblivion.

The road, mired and fissured,
caused chariots to falter and nobles to tumble.
As these cracks widened, no monarch dared traverse its length.
Eventually, the crevasses opened so vastly that the earth's fiery heart was
exposed, giving rise to a blazing fortress.
It was here that nobility and royalty sought refuge,
establishing a city known as Scorched Utopia.

A timid girl concealed herself from the night,
lighting every candle to fend off the darkness.
By day,
her dread of people confined her to shadows,
hoping to remain unseen at the street's edge.
The darkness eventually enveloped her,
pulling her into a realm where light ceased to exist.

In this domain, she confronted her fears
head-on and found they dissipated.
She realized her identity as Melinoe,
the progeny of Hades, in this revelation.

Alive

Mockery, mockery, the crowd's loud cry,
a plan so careful, a date so nigh.
The appointed hour, yet the vessel sways,
now veers away, sailing to a farther bay.

Toward the mountain up high,
toward confidence and away from strife.
In my grip, a hand so tight,
a snowy peak, on a luminous night.

Forgive the path once firmly set,
Spring's first drop, in neglect.
Forgive the bridge that bore a queen,
now twirling in a jester's scene.

Viridian land beneath us lies,
where tall pine trees splay before our eyes.
A mansion, once by fire consumed,
rebuilt from ashes, it bloomed.

Here stands a griffin, wings adorned with thorns,
with claws clenched, fortune was reborn.

To viridian land, a treasure brought,
a tale of revival, fervently wrought.

Ghost

I opened the dishwasher,
my gaze fixed on its fairest side.
It was dark,
and I am afraid of the dark.
I fear ghosts will emerge from the darkest corners.

I retreat and wash the dishes myself.
A voice behind me said,
"Fear not,
for I'm here to protect you."

I bring a soccer ball to the grassland.
The fresh scent of grass fills my nose.
I play happily
until I kick it so high it rolls to the side.
I trace it into a bush,
which hasn't felt the kiss of sunlight.
I reach my hand, then hold back,
for I am afraid of the darkness.
A voice behind me whispers,
"Fear not, I'll protect you."

I swim in the wild ocean,
enjoying the cool water on hot summer days.
I swim and swim until the greenish water turns dark blue.
The water beneath my feet feels not just cool
but cold and unreachable.

I want to swim back,
afraid of the dark and insecurity.
The beach is far from sight,
fading away,
but the voice murmurs,
"Fear not,
for I'm here for your safety."

This time, I see its face,
deep wrinkles emerging and
eyes so hollow they can't be traced.

It reaches out and shows me a black-framed card
with a transparent center.
"Grab this, place it in front of your eyes, and look through the transparent part."
I hold it.
The moment it touches me,
I find myself back at the sink, hands soapy with water.

I place the card in front of me.
A ghost emerges in the transparent card,
right there in the back of the dishwasher I was afraid of.
I place the card again on the bushes in the grassland.
Another ghost emerges and smiles at me.
I place it in the deep sea
and see a group of ghosts gathering on the ocean floor.

"I see the ghosts."
The moment I see them,
only the wrinkled man and I remain.
I feel a cold sensation around my neck.
The last words I hear are,
"Fear not, for I'm here for you."

I fall into dizziness
and wake surrounded by ghosts.
One holds a bowl, one holds a soccer ball, and one holds a fish.
The cold feeling on my neck is a knife cut,
and now it hurts no more.

"You saved me,"
I say to the ghosts.
They place the items beside me
and return me to my room.
I open my dishwasher and use it to wash my bowls.
I run back to the bushes and kiss them.
I swim back to the ocean and enjoy the coolness.

I soon realize
"the voice of protection ended my life."
The card could see the ghosts,
but the true foe was always the wrinkled-faced creature.
For I could see ghosts,
and they were the help.
Since then,
I fear darkness no more.

Apple Flower

The apple blossoms bloom in summer,
their stamens stretch out a little,
and their stems grow taller.
I see the petals expand,
their orange and red hues perfect for summer.
But I stop watering them
until they wither slowly.

The apple blossoms bloom in summer,
touched gently by bees,
admired by hummingbirds' fluttering wings,
bathed in a light spring rain.
Yet, I moved them from the backyard to my kitchen,
placed by the window,
so they could see nature from the inside,
but never feel it again.

The apple blossoms bloom in summer,
savoring the delicious soup's aroma,
stirred by the clear sound of cutting vegetables,
echoing the girl's footsteps.
I watch the petals wither,
questioning my actions.

The apple blossoms should bloom in summer,
their stems embrace sunlight,
their petals sing with tree shadows,
their stamens snoring under the gentle moonlight.
I should free the apple blossoms,
I am not the one who controls them,
I am not in control of them anymore.

Fortnight

May I say that the way you've grown is winding and intricate?
Like the spring river knocking pebbles loose along the shore
they tumble and blend
The fisherman discovers they are not mere fragments,
but precious minerals fused together.

May I say the way you live is elevated?
For you have witnessed falling stars form great caverns
and observed as clouds cast vast shadows over patchy fields.
You choose to dwell in the cave made by the fallen star,
drinking water that turns to rain on peaceful nights.
You use celestial stars as wishing machines,
hoping one day they will fulfill your dreams.

Can I say your world is chaotic?
For you have brought hot lava upon the rice fields,
night insects stop their songs in the face of withering crops and
hummingbirds clutch wormwood as they try to heal the land.
While you whisper the song of Elune,
the melancholy melody evokes the spirit of ancient pharaohs
and your eyes remain as still as ash.

The river brings hope to you,
the stars will shine bright for you,
the clouds will rain for you,
the glorious dream chases you.
You sleep,
And I wish you goodnight.

Shadow

I stare into the shadow
on a night baptized by cold wind.
The shadow seemed like a faithful friend—
I was so young, with untrained eyes.
The shadow was there with me,
and I, with it.

The moonlight bathed the world in its uneven glow,
and I got lost in the grand display of my thoughts.
Yet, in the dim light of the moon,
I couldn't see the true form of the shadow.

I grew up as the moonlight remained unchanged,
day after day, year after year.
A veil cast upon the earth whenever I looked,
but none were like the one I saw,
on that cold winter night.
I never looked back again.

I grew older and traveled further.
I saw the silhouette of a preying panther,
its black fur mingling with the shade—
too bloody to gaze upon.
I looked away from the shadow,
smelling a corpse near the panther,
its prey successfully taken.
I never looked back again.

I grew older and traveled further.
I saw a LaFerrari racing at Thunderhill track,
the red flags waving each passing car.
Their speed was dizzying,
yet the shade of the cars followed perfectly.

The roar of engines was too loud,
so, I shifted my gaze, staring blankly ahead.
Cheers erupted—

the winner must have claimed the prize,
but I never looked back again.

I grew older and traveled further.
I saw the godswood whispering legends of heroines,
its vast canopy casting a veil of darkness.
But the cold wind gnawed my bones—
the icy air too harsh to think of shadows.
I glimpsed a leaf falling,
its story untold as it sank into soil,
but I never looked back again.

I grew older and traveled further.
I sat by the Lushan Waterfall, howling ancient battles,
its droplets spreading traces like ink on a canvas.
A sudden splash soaked my shirt,
and I thought it best to stand back.
The thundering grew distant,
its flow never resting, never ceasing.
All its stone covered in slippery green moss.
But I never looked back again.

Yet I still remember my shadow,
the one that was with me—
the one that kept me company through moonlit nights,
the one that encouraged my soul with a silent stare.
The one that supported me when it heard me weep,
the one that blessed me when the moonlight disappeared.

I forgot where that shadow was cast,
and the memory of it grew blurry,
blended with my life's many shadows.
Those shadows may have been grander,
but none like the one that was with me.

It was the only shadow
daring to confront my soul,
daring to comfort my tears.

Now, at last, I look back—
back to the only shadow that stayed,
the only shadow I ever loved.

Dune

You are gone—
a specter beyond the physical,
withdrawn from the dimensions we once shared.
Your last step echoes on the solid earth,
your final parting words still linger.

Yet the warmth of your embrace clings to my skin;
the lessons you gave light my way through night and day.
Your gaze still meets my eyes and
your trust has seeped into the essence of my soul.
For I was the focus of your dedication
and the recipient of your boundless love.

I stand still—
feeling, recalling, reflecting.
Persistent in my longing rhymes,
addicted to the rhythms of memory,
relentless in the pursuit of dreams,
shaped immeasurably by your influence.

Though you are gone from the physical realm,
our souls remain intricately entwined,
waltzing on the icy lake beyond the material,
enduring, passing through the eternal.

Oath

Raindrops share tales heard beneath the pine tree,
whispering of which raindrop finds her rainbow.
As they gather and gather,
a storm begins to form.
Since then, people have started to flee,
no longer praising the loving raindrops on the crops
but fleeing and cursing the storm.

Love joyously assembles,
debating which children they cherish,
speaking of books read under the balcony,
spreading love stories, inspiring belief in fairytales.
They gather and gather
until love grows heavy like chains.
The prince cries out for freedom and
abandons his vows.
Since then,
love has dissipated into the air,
touching only those who breathe.

The wind blows, bringing a soft breeze to the girl,
embracing runners after their strenuous races,
drying their sweat and easing their fatigue.
The wind gathers until a tornado forms.
Then, the runners begin to blame the tornado
for halting their competition.
The medals they were meant to receive are reluctantly retracted.

Orchard

Go into any grassland,
or backyard—just anywhere that has a tree,
whether tall or short, thick or thin.

If it's short, lower your body until you are shorter than it.
If it's tall, great, you don't have to waste time bowing.

Look up, and you'll see branches with layers.
The lower ones, we can easily reach to pluck a leaf.
The taller ones require a small jump.
The highest may even need a ladder.

But—
whether from a tall or short branch
they all aim for the ground.
So, if you want a fresh leaf,
why not wait for it to come to you?

The little child lies in the orchard with her eyes closed,
waiting for a falling leaf.
The sun, hidden behind a cloud, casts a shadow over her.
She opens her eyes, sensing sudden darkness—
oh, it's the leaf covering her eyes, not the sun behind the clouds.

She closes her eyes again and dreams.
In them, all memories return,
and the boy sitting beside her
reaches out his hand in invitation.

She is so excited that the dream fades as she opens her eyes.
And the moment she does,
the orchard trees are not just leafy—
but now are heavy with fresh fruit.

The boy waves under a tree,
holding a big watermelon, inviting her:
"It's time to eat!"

Oh, this is more than just a dream.

Youth

I count to four,
One, two, three, four——
"Here is the ticket for the movie."
The boy hands it to the girl.
They sit in the middle of the theater,
sharing the same box of popcorn.

I count to four,
One, two, three, four——
Here are the letters she wrote to him,
handwritten, one for each of a hundred days.
The girl gives them to the boy,
carefully wrapped in a charcoal-colored box.

I count to four,
One, two, three, four——
"The answer is three, not four."
The boy smiles, his gaze is fixed on the girl,
teaching her equations beneath a wisteria arbor
the summer sun turned his hair a soft brown.

I count to four,
One, two, three, four——
This ticket is for him,
though he won't be at her graduation.
She still writes his name on the blank ticket.
The girl holds the fourth ticket in her hand,
his name is prewritten, though the seat remains empty.
With the ticket in hand,
he is already with her.

First Love

It was a swamp, small and shallow,
as she was young and naïve.
Her smile, wide and bright, illuminated her imagination.

She jumped into the swamp,
muddy spots staining her white skirt.
The swamp expanded,
and in a second, she was sinking deeper.
She called for freedom.

He came with a stick,
thin and fragile, as if it would break any moment.
Yet, she caught it and
climbed from the swamp.

Free, she looked into his eyes—
hazel, reflecting her muddy face.
The road cleared ahead,
stretching farther than she could feel.

At the crossroad, she leaped forward and
turned to face him,
the stick still in his hands,
the obstacles now cleared by the weapon that saved her.

He waved his now calloused hands
turned his back
never turning back again.

Guardian

Some grass clings to life in narrow cracks,
whispering why it wasn't the rose tendered by the Little Prince.
Yet other blades bow in gratitude,
thankful for a quiet patch of earth that holds them close.
They cannot see the rain gathering, waiting to nourish,
nor know they will one day stand as towering trees,
guardians of this rich and silent land.

The tree loves the soil that once embraced it,
cherishes that small refuge for a lifetime,
grateful for its gentle nurture, bound to its memory.
For that tiny patch of earth has woven itself
into every ring, every root, every vein of the tree.

Now the tree grows tall, its gaze lost in the skies,
no longer held close to the soil as it was when just a tender blade.
Yet every fruit it bears is an offering, a tribute,
to the soil that once cradled its fragile roots.

Awaken

Why does the willow need a hand to straighten its boughs?
It bathes in sunlight, combs through rain,
draws nourishment from all it needs.

Why does an arrow require a bow to fell a boar?
We cast spears with our hands,
and still, we claim the bear as our prey.

Why does the weight of a man's heavy armor join the fray?
We can win our glories with hair softly stirred by the breeze,
honors placed upon our crowns.

Why seek a reason to let our feelings fly?
We can run beside the Mississippi,
whispering ancient lore from the days of Rome.

When summer's scorching waves approach,
there's no need to point; the sun is already high above.